ıangle

Tangle

Julie Cameron Gray

TIGHTROPE BOOKS

Tightrope Books
17 Greyton Crescent
Toronto, Ontario. M6E 2G1
www.tightropebooks.com

Edited by Jim Johntone
Typography by Dawn Kresan
Cover design by Nathaniel G. Moore
Author photograph by Guy Crawford

Printed and bound in Canada

We thank the Canada Council for the Arts, the Ontario Arts
Council, and the Government of Ontario through the book
publishing tax credit for their support of our publishing program.

Canada Council   Conseil des Arts   ONTARIO ARTS COUNCIL   Ontario
for the Arts   du Canada   CONSEIL DES ARTS DE L'ONTARIO   Ontario Media Development Corporation

Library and Archives Canada Cataloguing in Publication

Gray, Julie Cameron
      Tangle / Julie Cameron Gray.

POEMS.
ISBN 978-1-926639-57-4

      I. TITLE.

PS8613.R3877T35 2013   C811'.6   C2013-901864-6

for J.

TABLE OF CONTENTS

I

After a Stage Performance of *Anna Karenina*   13
In response to 'What's new?'   14
Never: Red Fable   15
Ultramarine   16
At a Cottage in a Wireless Dead Zone   17
Mowing the Lawn, Sunday   18
A Country Pub in Avon   20
Your Parka Trimmed in Fur   21
Application to the Art Deco Society of California   22
The Last Blonde on Earth   23

II

Confessions of a Workaholic   27
Ode to the French Phrase-a-Day Desk Calendar   28
Ode to the Computer Mouse   29
Ode to the Stapler   30
Viral   32
Limited Vocabulary   33

III

Saffron: Five Poems   37
Wasp Nest: The Theory of Multiple Continuity   42
Black, White and Red All Over   43
Breakfast in your Mother's Kitchen   44
How to Fail   46
Parallel Lives   48

IV

Newlywed   53

Coordinating Geometry: Various Realities...   54

My Type of Man   58

Reasons Why You Are Not Good Enough   59

If You Lived Here, You'd be Home by Now   60

Widow Fantasies   62

I Can See Now That I Never Really Loved Any Of You   65

V

Ultramarine II   69

Young Men on Rollerblades   71

The Commuter's Elimination Dance   72

Haiku for Penguins in a Box   74

Seventeen   75

A Young Housewife Considers Baking   76

Dinner Party   77

Driving to Sudbury at Night   78

Expatriate   79

There Are No Pretty Girls Here   80

NOTES   83

ACKNOWLEDGEMENTS   84

AUTHOR BIOGRAPHY   85

I

After a Stage Performance of *Anna Karenina*

Ugly, unloved month. How
partial I am to the muddy clouds,

the concrete defining your sightline.
Stone planter, cement steps—

you would be marble in the sun.
Already you're only enduring,

the quick night curled in the sling
of your scarf. Slip a small coin

down a magic slot and hear
whatever you have to say

come rattling from your mouth.
Surfeit, these graphite branches,

these swanlike skies of November.
Take my ears, completely,

haul them back through a Russian
Pastoral, a theatre in St. Petersburg.

Drag me through a wedding ring,
a dark velvet train.

In response to 'What's new?'

The sky was pale all day, bright and sunless.
I woke up with a hairpin still in my hair, studded
with purple glass. I slipped it under my pillow.
I've been spending my days floundering in a cabin in the woods,
drinking gin and tonic, singing along to the radio.
I make eyes at the out-of-season ladybugs that cling
to the inside windows, scaling their private glaciers.
The deer leave their shadowed footprints across
my front door; I almost hit one driving into town for bread.
There are snowshoes leaning their Eiffeled bodies
against the door frame, at night the sunsets
are a shock of fuchsia. Then there are bare
branches, the black spruces, and at night
I dream of aqueducts and powdered sand.
Other than that, nothing is new.
The sky was pale, all day.

Never: Red Fable

I will want once: forest
and a robin's breast.
The cabin was always empty,
always waiting for this.
Overripe berries fill my hands,
but *no*, you say,
you'll never eat, never drink,
although I'll want twice, and then
seed, stem, leaf-
rip the skin off a pomegranate,
red flash inside. Hint and sharpen--
who is wolf, teeth. Are there claws?
Being eaten, meat of a cherry,
being drink and carried drunk.
I'll come ran, come kissed,
riding the empty bed.
Never for a mouth crushed with roses.
Never wolf, never red cape, have and having
to which I want to say, hoodless,
again and again and again, lick
the edges of red absence from your lips,
and you'll want twice,
and then—
gently if you can.
You will never be this red again.

Ultramarine

Ultramarine saddles up to the bar, offers to buy you a drink. You're already drinking a glass of ultramarine, but it won't leave you alone. As it drones on endlessly about how unlike ultramarine the local government has been, your mind wanders off a cliff to cannonball into the deep. It survives, miraculously, buoyed by the sudden appearance of a beach ball, sponsored by ultramarine. You go back to your hotel and find the room empty, your suitcase gone, and a letter addressed to ultramarine in which your father lists the disappointments that have been tallied in the off hours of sleeplessness. You are running late for a conference, the whole reason you came here in the first place. Settling into your seat, you scan the conference information packet and find that the keynote speaker is addressing the crowd on the tax benefits of ultramarine. You sneak out early to go back to your room, take a shower. The shower stream feels like a thousand elbows on a packed subway train, ready to pour out at the next station, Ultramarine.

At a Cottage in a Wireless Dead Zone

I should either learn to keep
my mouth shut or give
it nova-bright flares. You
would burn the transcripts

of our late nights in this bedroom,
the attic. Would we be better off?
If a lacework of fir trees and light
brings on nostalgia like this,

then I should have stayed in the city,
its fermata of please. Could, really.
Rather than standing here, tethered
to a dark cloud of roaming data

clean as binary,
and this new kind of mean.

Mowing the Lawn, Sunday

At first we believed in the immutability
of the white farmhouse, the snow
and the blue windows, the pot of husked
daffodils visible from the outside.
Inside, the dining room table
was a sea maps, mugs of cold
tea became islands locked
against it like snow
locks on window panes,
white melting moths.
When spring came it was easier to see
the cliff where the lawn dropped away
to a small valley, where magnolia trees
were shedding their white gloves.

Now, the grass is high enough to warrant
a careful steering of the mower
to the green lip, avoiding the drop
where the previous owner was pulled
by the weight of the mower and snapped
his neck when he hit the bottom.
His wife's grief: silent, stunned-fawn
shock, as she sat in the closed garage
running their old Mazda with the windows down
until she was found, days later.
Not that there aren't neighbours,
but the real estate advertises acres of land,

and acres are what you get.
They have to tell you things like that
when you buy a place. I am unbothered.

I've been slowly reworking the drop,
filling the hollow at the bottom with clean fill,
leveling off the top to a gentle slope.
We walk to the edge some evenings
and talk about what it will look like
when it's done, if the strange lights
or the movement that you sometimes
see out of the corner or your eye will stop.
When you go to the shops
and leave me a list of chores
I wait for what seems like days,
and the floor folds itself into origami birds,
samurai hats, stars with many points.
I stand at the crest of the drop and look
down, see my own body there.
The lawn mower smashed, jagged
and dangerous even when broken.

A Country Pub in Avon

We stood outside an Austen-era farm-manor-turned-pub
crumbling against the climbing roses,
the lead glass windows arched and diamonding.
Beyond the low stone wall, the lichen-frosted ledge,
the green rolls on to the grey limits of Bristol.
A man fitting your description

drove past. The angle of your profile, your hands
on the wheel, the seven buttons down the front
of your shirt. I brushed against the nettles
in surprise – my leg burning for hours afterwards.
I imagined I wrote you a long, slow letter
transcribed on the side of a rabbit.

Except it is more like this—we spend the day
picking cider apples by the side of the highway,
see a rabbit transformed into a thin sheet
of fur and nothing more. I lean against your shoulder
for a photograph: confidence. All its meanings.
The light went deep yellow in the afternoon.

Your Parka Trimmed in Fur

We are surrounded by milky coffee
steaming out of cups on white saucers.
A bit of bread, blackberry jam.
Gloves float by the cafe window, carried
off in gold leaf clouds. Which means
it may snow. All afternoon
we admired the white hands
of basil flowers growing on the windowsill,
learning an argot of short grey light.

Underground, we ride from one bar
to the next. I'm admiring your parka
trimmed in fur, your hair falling
in smooth dark waves over the hood.
A flood of fluorescence is strapped
to the ceiling, highlights each
tile on every stair to street level.
There is a parade above us: the sky
throws handfuls of snowflakes
and even the winds are a marching band,
now that they've found all the vowels
we contain.

Application to the Art Deco Society of California

Condensation drips off a cool glass of gin,
drops onto the perfect green lawn
of a summer afternoon,
with all the prettiest people playing
their best flappers and philosophers,
dressed up for cocktails.

Misplaced dancing shoes,
bootlegged booze; the moment
in sequined sheath
when I can no longer stand
the sound of his laugh.
The only solution is the Charleston
and more drinks.

The silver notes of band brass
and bass cling to air
and slowly give way to dusk—

champagne and stars soar drunk
in a pollen-flecked swimming pool.

The Last Blonde on Earth

Sunlight stretches out
on white sheets, her hair
a yellow froth.

You would give up your name
and the names of everyone
you've ever met to stay here,
where the sunlight flecks the flaws
from everything it touches.

A blue bowl of apricots
on the bedside table.

Her field bright fingernails
painted aureate gold.

II

Confessions of a Workaholic

Sometimes when I'm in the car
staring across achromatic snowfields,
dried stalks of prairie grass,
and all I want is to come home,
it's you I think of.

Where you are not an email, a name
floating across a computer screen
or the blinking red on my cell phone
that might well be a light
flashing across the harbour.

But no sweetheart, I can't say
it happens all that often.

Ode to the French Phrase-a-Day Desk Calendar

Darling, with your jaunty squared-
off stance, French akimbo,

your ribbon of text parading by my
tired eyes and boredom-stilled

mind, I'm suddenly aware of my own
heart beating. You know the salt

taste of desire, the urge for something
more—after all, your kingdom

is made of promise, *je ne sais quoi,*
all the acreage you can claim

to the right of my computer screen.
Quand est-ce que vous partez?

I ask of you, whispering
in the pillow talk of the day.

J'ai d'autres projets, you say.
J'ai promis à une seule année.

Ode to the Computer Mouse

Ergonomic, your body is a hall of mirrors—
the red light inside you ricocheting, searching
for direction. My hand knows your back,
your meagre pair of buttons,
your scrolling spine.
I've held you so much your body
has pocks of camouflage,
rashes of hand cream.
Stark and struck dumb, I compass
your red eye around the world wide,
fold my fingers over your plastic jacket.
Waltz you around the dance floor
of this mouse pad. The well
where my thumb rests,
the waist of your slim self.
You are the small black bird of my days.

Ode to the Stapler

Star of my arsenal, general
of pens and stray post-its:
you are at ease
amoung the vast field
of my desk.

Each morning you wait.
The endless
white tide
yields to you alone.

I know you so well—
the small mechanical
theatre of your noble
body, the music
of your spring pulled taut

ready to load while
my hand holds your beige
angles deftly and I slide
a tidy row of slivered steel
into your mouth.

Oh stapler! It's you
and me, on a mission
to keep every white thing
together, bound
by the small steel
bite of your law.

Viral

Spreads like Swedish furniture, like Starbucks, like the English language. Steals over, creeps on its toes over the creaking hardwood, sneaks up, saddles up, two steps, entrechats. Kneels down in the warm soil and plants its dark seeds and waits for them to take root. Blooms, unfurls, sprouts hoary little legs. Mushrooms, fans out, invades, shoots; goes fishing, comes back with dinner. Arrives wrapped as a gift and waits until the city falls asleep, so it can spring out and infect every citizen it comes across. Announces that you simply must watch this YouTube video. Erupts in a lava of criticism about your friends, haircut, shoes, and reading habits. Collects the small secrets and loose change of your body, builds an aerie in the hollow of your shoulder blade, and begins to write its memoirs.

Limited Vocabulary

Think of it as verb for being
somewhere you shouldn't,
as another word for rehearsing
the right thing to say
after the moment to say it has passed.
Think of it as a crushed fig,
a small plane crash, a woman rolling her eyes.
Think of another word for this.
Look at the streetlights turning into fireflies
and tell me you don't know what you're doing.
Think of another word for what you're doing.
Think of another word for the hollows of your body,
for the strands of hair that have fallen
from your scalp and cling to your sweater.
Think of a word that is the sum
of what we've burned.
A word that searches
for something outside of you
that makes you more yourself.
Think of it.
Think of it as___.
Make up a word if you have to.

III

Saffron: Five Poems

The Saffron Gatherers

A scale heaped with the last dried
rays of sunset against solid brass bells.
150 volatile, aroma-yielding compounds—
dried fireworks, a hay of shredded red.
Each morning you bend, pry open
the purple lock of petals
and pluck three threads inside.
The scent of honey, your yellow hand,
your body hunched in the early
light that turns the sky a field
of blue water, white waterlilies.
The bed of purple nails beneath
your hands, pressing you on.

The Non-Culinary Uses of Saffron

A pound of saffron buys a horse or a wife;
your daughter's hand weighed out
in the red fur of pure colour worth
more than salt. The Romans floated
saffron in wine to stave off hangovers, slept
on pillows stuffed with dried stamens.
A German physician proposed it could cure the plague,
toothaches, and when combined with crushed
snails and earthworms, jaundice.
When you kill your wife, burn all the dried gold
in the city to demonstrate your grief—
saffronize the past
until it glows clean as a knife.

Safranschau
—Germany, 1374

The saffron inspectors have found false
alchemy: saffron cut with marigold petals,
safflower, beet fibers. The dealer is dragged
by horse through the streets, gutted
until his entrails spill like soup from a bowl
and then buried, the crowd hopes
while still alive, his mouth stuffed
with small bags of the adulterated gold
he tried so desperately to sell.
Three others are burned alive for peddling
cut saffron, and each time the pyre stoked
with the hay of their wares. Witnesses spoke
of it as the most beautiful fire—
in turn the colour of custard, carrot,
egg yolk, the silkiest domestic fox
that had ever been.

The Crocus Dreams of the Lake District

My red threads are the hair of a Titian
beauty queen, an armful of tiger lilies
put through a shredder. Float them in a bowl
of water—turns yellow as a finch throat.
I am as separate as a ghost, a stone from a quarry.

Daffodils bloom untouched on the green
shores of Ullwater, a lake lit by lamps.
There, a royal ceremony of yellow robes,
a plague of chatty finches upon thrones.

The Crocus as Lewis Carroll

The crocus has come to town. It's at the Savoy
in a room full of blue moths, thinking of you.

There, the crocus is writing its last letters.
It begins each with *my dearest heart*

and none are sent. It fingers the curtains,
shreds its purple crown as the days grow

long and moody, and the cello calls
for its resignation, holds three ribbons

of orange light for ransom. The crocus
is a silkworm, the calf that will be veal.

(My dearest heart: I see a crocus in your hair,
a crocus on your brow. Your heart, a crocus...)

The crocus stalks you, still.

Wasp Nest: The Theory of Multiple Continuity

Tessellated, a new day drones.
The queen begins with what
she knows—polytopes, wood fibre,
Euclidean geometry—a flawless
building shaped by hexagon
upon hexagon upon hexagon.
It's the same with kitchen tile—polytopic,
small rooms in our separate kingdoms.

Our homes are not so different.
O unpublished road map
of n-dimensional space, blueprint
of faultless colonized minds—
I'm trussed in the exoskeletal
bodice of your favourite yellow jacket.

Black, White and Red All Over

There are birds
and there are cages, but they don't always
come in pairs. Rubber boots, thick
and necessary, with rain and your red coat.

The rain and your red coat and the red
phone booth. There is a lovely
little wolf and four numbers
to count the blocks from his door.
Black door, white
door, checkerboard floor.
Shirt, check. The red coat slipped
off the back of a chair, into a pretty
puddle on the black and white tiles.

A line drawing, pen and ink,
a moustache being twirled. Red birds
that have never known cages, never
known the loneliness of the coat
left in the kitchen after we moved
to the bedroom. Black boots
on a newspaper by the door,
a lovely little wolf
curled up on the floor.

Breakfast in Your Mother's Kitchen

Scientific American while I eat toast,
drink coffee. I am reading about time,

the nature of it, trying not to watch
the blue delphiniums lose their petals,

which limp, then drop and stick on the white
counter. The nature of the colour blue.

The scent is a complex cylinder
of round things, of undiscovered cures

for undiscovered cancers.
You are outside, painting

the house the colour of egg yolk,
split wide, bent on consuming

the frying pan. I can hear her
moving around upstairs,

she has retreated to somewhere
unpleasant. I hear her

sighing continuously. The article
in *Scientific American* is

"How to Build a Time Machine",
were such lendings of light and speed

possible. Upstairs your mother uses
photographs, a record of time

and light, to move from minutes
into decades, memories slowly

boiled down and sugared
like the jam on the counter.

How to Fail

"To love is to be remarkable, and flawless.
It is to wear the yellow crowns of all the gods."
—Gwendolyn MacEwen

Say that you have all the time in the world,
there's no rush. Say that it's only one drink,
one night, one kiss; then talk to too loudly
about what you do for a living. Drive too fast
on roads you don't know well. Coast,
the verb you live by.

To fail is to wear the yellow crown
of all the gods nobody can remember.
Fail, the hours you spent watching TV
when you meant to write your novel.
Fail, the woman you thought would deliver you
yet sucked your hours through a straw.
Then it will be summer, your back wet with sweat,
and rain sometimes falls into your drink on
the patio and you call it love. Every song that plays
is meant just for you. Then it will be winter
and nothing has changed except your shirt
and the weather.

Then another winter, and another,
until no one remembers when winters began.
The patio's closed, the songs repeat
and you know all the words—
but tomorrow things are going to change.
You'll buy orange juice, update
your resume, exercise, do the laundry.
This time it will be different, you can feel it.

Parallel Lives

It's suspicious, waking before the alarm.

Last night it rained, and now
the odds are even better

that a jogger or dog walker
will discover a body clumsily folded

into a garbage bag. Though right now
it's only me, with no plans

to leave the house, imagining
someone else's tragedy.

Through the window, trees appear
to have sharpened their branches

overnight, as though the branch-sharpening
van has come by with its jingling tune and slow,

pedophilic pace. Above me, pipes rattle
and water rushes from somewhere. It's only

a matter of time until the mysterious dripping
proves just how insidious tiny sounds can be.

May it be years from now,
the headache of a carved apart ceiling, pried

back like ribs to display the shining
interior hiding behind the stucco

curtain of civility. You know that it's coming.
It wants to show how alike

you've been, all these years.

IV

Newlywed

The back alleys bloomed night flowers of graffiti,
those marched-up days when the open window filled
our bedroom with grey cloud and damp pavement.
Half awake, eyes closed, arms reaching through the sonar
of blankets, as though the artificial down of an Ikea duvet
were a mermaid of polyester we both wished to hold.
I blame the hyacinths, their purple jazz-hands
kick-ball-changing their perfume through the window frame.
Here in the well-charted provinces, the subdivisions
backend busy shop streets, hitched and tethered.
Already the climbing ivy is pulling at the brickwork,
working a monogram into these rented walls.
Let's never get out of bed. Let's just be still and slow
and take in the damp salt near the window,
your surname a new adjective, our breathing
a sea locked in a shell; the stealthy hyacinths, invading
scent first, counting the weeks since the wedding.

Coordinating Geometry: Various Realities in the Hypothesis of Encounter

Prologue: We Met Through Friends

Let me explain:
two lines, moving.
Variously,
 you are the line (l)
and I am the point (p)
but there are differing degrees
of parallelism, the way
some lines encounter others
as though a surface plane
could extend without end
in all directions.
Wait here. I'll get a pencil.

i. Euclidean: Diagrams on a Cocktail Napkin

In parallels, all right angles
are equal. Also: things that coincide
equal one another. You and I,
but it didn't seem true then.
Here is a circle without radius—
one exists, but we can't draw it yet.
We deal in circumference
waiting for diameter.
We assert the existence of objects
without revealing how to construct them.
Here is a compass—it isn't much,
but it's a start.

ii. Hyperbolic: Bookstore

(l) and (l) do not intersect,
(p) is a bookstore.
Instead of leaving my coffee
I finished it, demonstrated the importance
of fractal seconds by missing the next bus,
then read the first five pages
of Down and Out in London and Paris
twenty minutes after you
had done the same.
Any other lines of interest (l)
are ultra-parallel to you
and will never intersect (p).
So you see, a line segment cannot
be scaled up indefinitely. Result:
we went without rain for weeks.

iii. Elliptic: Bedroom, Early Morning

Your hands through my hair, fingers
through tangled wires.
Here there are no parallels—
(l) passes through (p).
The interior sum of our angled limbs
is always more than one hundred
and eighty degrees. Meaning:
there is no looking back.
But no looking forward, either.
This is the viewpoint favoured
by passengers in cars
as towns, trees, and transformers
are bisected by pavement.
A car hydroplaning a road.
Every angle the desire
to make our own luck,
and extend without end
in all directions.

My Type of Man

I have a weakness for blue-eyed asthmatics who are allergic to cats, for failed musicians, for both men with good jobs and men with no jobs, a weakness for addictive personalities, for addicts in general, for older men mostly, for men who I wish were smarter than me but aren't, men who like the idea of my writing more than the writing itself, whose reading habits are deplorable once they stop trying to impress me, men who drink too much and tell me they love me too soon, who are selective in their morals, men who cook, who own passports and know how to use them, who are earnest and shameless when trying to win my heart, for former teenage geeks, for men whose mothers will never love me but propose marriage anyway, for both the romantically impaired and the serial monogamists, men who feel that no one really understands them or drives as well as they do, and when they are driving they sing along to the radio and the sun through the windshield has warmed the skin on their arms and there are easy silences between us, I fall for them every single time.

Reasons Why You Are Not Good Enough

Tea bag squeezer, nickel tickler, doorknob fondler,
teeth gnasher, spider killer, eye roller, undertipper,
finger flipper, re-gifter, pronunciation corrector,
distracted driver, lousy dresser, limp handshaker,
debbie downer, dumpster diver, seagull feeder,
over-the-shoulder reader, wing clipper, always chipper,
fancy baker, smile faker, twitchy trigger, affection trifler,
parade rainer, long winded toaster, unwanted suitor,
punch buggy puncher, over quaffer, parking lot puker,
public relations peddler, health nut nagger, husband dazzler,
conversation crippler, self-described scholar,
hard luck bawler, selfish lover, needy bugger.

If You Lived Here, You'd be Home by Now

All I can remember is we talked, that I saw
your room and the bed was low

with a rumpled grey duvet. A friend said: *it's been years
since you saw him, dreams are funny like that.*

But it happened again. I think of you.
I think of you and wonder, how could we know?

Just the usual failures, invisible from the outset:
an imagined future curdled into a standoff,

your indifference a joke I wasn't getting.
After walking myself home too many nights,

luckless, tugging my jacket tight around my body—
I should have said, *no*. I should have said, *something else.*

Now, I imagine you in the shower, rivulets
of soap down your runner's legs.

Maybe sometimes you wake up surprised
to find my voice locked away in sleep.

There, my face is still in its twenties
and the mouthfuls are fearless;

before the collapsed pleura
of quiet, the disbanding of air.

Widow Fantasies

I want my husband to disappear, dissolve
like a spoonful of sugar in a cup of coffee.

I want him to fall asleep at the wheel,
for a distracted driver to make a mistake,
for snow to conceal a slippery surface.
I want it quick and painless and over in a flash.
Twist of metal, bone, the shattered
windshield a constellation
across black ice.
Traffic backed up for miles.

I'd get a call in the night, some
official telling me *so sorry ma'am,
but your husband…*
I want to know that grief.

And then my husband would be perfect,
a perfection that exists only in absence.

I imagine the funeral, where I'd be buffered
on all sides by my family, by his—
I would be small, suffering, mute,
barely able to stand the funeral service.

The clucking of tongues:
He was so young.
Such a shame they never had children.
And underneath it all:
But she's young, she'll find another.

My husband:
Lost like a letter in the mail,
a button off a coat.

And the absence—
how exquisite to be burdened and alone
with that misery, a wound
so clean.

I imagine moving about my apartment,
fingering his belongings, crying
I never wanted this to happen, I never
really meant it. It was just a thought.

But at night in my big empty bed
the stars would claw at my window,
branches would scratch at the glass,
saying *you wanted this.*

I would know it was the desire,
the brief fantasy that gave me
this precise and measured loss,
dispatched as coolly as life insurance.
But it isn't money I want,
when I imagine my husband gone forever—

No, it's the delicious cut of the tie,
the severing,
as clean as a head from a body.

I Can See Now That I Never Really Loved Any of You

I imagine you all in a boardroom, fluorescently lit,
discussing me as though at an awkward book club.
I'm amazed you've come, to clear your throats
and watch your fantasies dissolve—
those who brought armloads of old letters,
folded evidence of feeling no longer
felt; please place them in the tray on the left.

I can see now that I never really loved any of you.
All right, maybe a couple, but look around—
can you guess which ones? The little patter
is smaller than what we once shared, but still bangs
its hooves in the stall. Do you feel that
ache of nostalgia or hate? Can you tell which ones
love me more for leaving? And the ones that want
me dead, or at least begging… this is not what you expected.
You wanted to gather up the days we had
by the corners, lift those perfect moments
when we were flawless out of the miserable ash,
and daisy chain them together as though you can
cancel out loss. That's not going to happen.
Here there are no overdue speeches, no parting
shots for any of you.

My icebergs, dressed in flannel, against the backdrop of cafes
and white coffee cups, after all the money had been spent.
Geography and my Goldilocks approach to your ambitions.
There are no exit interviews, nothing more to be had.
It's just me, looking you all over through one-way
glass, with my forensic indifference for the vulpine
teeth you've just begun to notice.
Can you really be surprised?
I am exactly as I always was.

V

Ultramarine II

—Eleuthera, Bahamas

Every day the water and sky competed for Best in Blue,
and when you drank enough the whole day was cobalt.
You got used to dizziness, the water always
in front of you. Sometimes you put down your drink,
picked up a book and pen, but always the drink again.
Slices of yellow stars. Glass sweating in your hand.

Her earring: silver lure and a bullet of lapis.
You said, don't wear jewellery, it attracts sharks.
She laughed, bobbed her head under.
Her hair Opheliaed and your mouth leaned forward
as if swallowing the air in the space she once was.

You stare down the water and sky until they refuse to separate—
even when you go to get another drink
and look back, there they are, seamless
in a way you have never been with anyone.
You lie back, the sun through your transparent eyelids
is a red haze, but you wish it were ultramarine.

There is sand in your bed. The night comes and bends
over your sheet strewn body, star-flung and feverish.
You hear the surf outside your window; get up for a glass
of water. A glimpse of yourself in the bathroom mirror
and you aren't sure what you're looking at.

You stayed through New Years, dressed in black tie,
and beyond the gates local children
set off bottle rockets in the street.
White flares popped like gunfire.
At the party, you admired the orchids, smoked cigars.
When the champagne gave way to sparkling wine,
no one knew the difference. You stumbled
to the bathroom, lamenting loudly
that the stars were gone, we had consumed them all.
Steadying yourself against the sink,
you searched the mirror for something
you were sure was missing, anything
to make you bear another day here
but found only yourself,
drowning in ultramarine.

Young Men on Rollerblades

Some wax the clean edge
of concrete that holds
marigolds, careful lettering
of a business tower address. Others
sit on the pavement and lean back
like lizards in the new season's sun.
They take turns leaping up and grinding down
the ledge, their feet precisely
placed as though expecting a dance
partner to fall out of the atmosphere
and join them as they slingshot back.

Lithe acrobats taking to the sky like Icarus
and gliding back to earth
down a metal handrail.
Some land perfectly and sail calmly
across slate grey, others collapse
into split lips, coconut cracked knees.
Hurling themselves through the air
lengthwise and cocksure:
knees bent, ready for the next
bluff against gravity.

Here's another coming now,
shot through an invisible catapult,
swimming through the clear blue air.
Wheels and concrete connect, hold sure.

THE COMMUTER'S ELIMINATION DANCE

All those who think guerrilla theatre is a legitimate activity on a subway.

Anyone who has travelled in costume, either going to or coming from a re-enactment of a war, real or fictional.

Anyone who eats multiple butterscotch pudding cups while in transit, and places each peeled off lid pudding-side-down on their pants.

Anyone who feels smug about reading books via an e-reader.

The woman who I once sat next to and engaged me in a silent but somewhat painful match of Whose Elbow Can Press Most Aggressively into the Other's Elbow.

Anyone who listens to music on their cell phone without earphones, forcing everyone within 20 feet to listen to a tinny, wretched version of some popular teen song.

Anyone who has cried openly, but held a blurry book so that people would think it was a deeply moving novel.

Those that read self-help books on the train with overly-sharing titles such as, 'How to Trick a Rich Man into Marrying You', or "When Murder isn't an Option: How to Control your Anger".

Anyone who has tripped another with their ridiculous briefcase on wheels.

Any man that has deliberately sat with their legs spread so far apart that it's impossible for someone to sit in the seat beside them.

Anyone who has spent an entire commute wondering if the woman standing is pregnant. If not, she would be offended if you offered her your seat; If so she likely is already offended because no one had offered her a seat.

Anyone who has searched the tunnel-dark for a diamond as big as The Ritz.

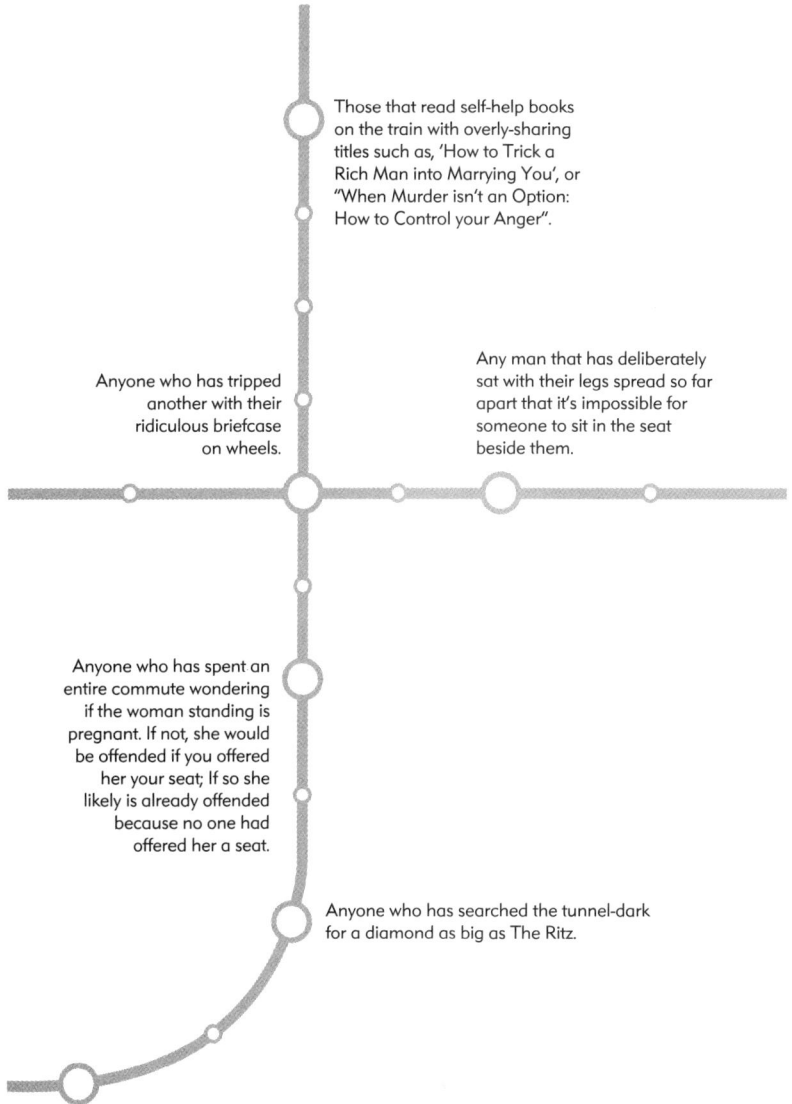

All those who stand still on escalators, waiting for the mechanical stairs to ferry them up.

73

Haiku for Penguins in a Box

A box of old penguin books—
slim volumes of orange
and pale green, classics.

The corners rounded into velvet
well-thumbed, well-pocketed,
so loved.

Where are your first owners,
the ones that chose you new
off a shelf, one spring?

Now huddled in a crate
like kittens, under a bright
winter sun.

Oh little treasures
come home with me today—
you are better than new.

Seventeen

It was the year of bestseller junkie narrative,
hardcore romance, the epic and unreal.
She even dragged around blockbuster
hardcovers; stacked them in her locker.
You watched her carefully: found
yourself obsessing over a single
blue thread tethered
to the cuff of her sleeve.

Your stomach a low hanging knot,
wanting to feel her mouth
on yours, her hands on your back, twisting
your shirt into flowers in her fists.
You even read the books she read,
wanted to know what you had to do.
Save the girl. Carry her through rain.
If only you could be that rescuer,
have that slow motion moment,
complete with a brand new
soundtrack by your favourite band.

But you know it's the same old story:
Everyone reads the book,
sees the movie.
No one in real life
can ever measure up.

A Young Housewife Considers Baking

She scans directions and studies pictures
Of cakes, tarts, pies and pastries—
the instructions read like a fable
as she marches through step aerobics
in her living room. Her legs pull
themselves left up down right
across the plush carpet and back again.
She thinks of the shining tin tower
of baking sheets and cake moulds
stacked in the kitchen, selects recipes
as carefully as planning her children's
future, and insists
she will buy ingredients tomorrow.
Her waist grows smaller and smaller,
a wet sugar cube.
She's wheat free, dairy free, calorie reduced
and shriveling like a plum in the sun.
Nothing anyone can say out loud
that the sinews of her body haven't
already written.
Just a bit more, she says.
Just a bit more and then it will be enough.

Dinner Party

You squeeze a lime slice into my drink, stab
at the ice with the measly cocktail straw.
To be a thing, a person, a *here*,
pretending you're young and there aren't
children sleeping upstairs with mouths open
and their limbs flung wide, dreaming dark
complex dreams beyond their vocabularies.
Are they not you? Vapour of lime wafting everywhere,
laughing too loudly and dizzy, dizzy with mouthfuls
of clear, clean noise. Juniper, gash
of recognition—realizing you're
drunk and denying it.

See how far we've come:
the drinks, the good lighting, a well-fitting shirt—
yet already a few are gathering
up their coats, hoisting sleep-addled
children into car seats, slamming doors.
Driving with the vents on even though
the heating hasn't kicked on yet.

Your wife admired the host's hands,
they are woven baskets, handsome lyrics to a song
sung through lines and lines of laundry, hung in some
summered backyard in a season unlike this one.
The revelation seeping into your skin like meltwater,
maybe you didn't get her first.

Driving to Sudbury at Night

Jackpines shelter. The guardrail nothing
more than a line of soldiering logs, driven
into the edge of the road and connected
by steel wire. The sky on my right is the long
line of an event horizon, or a ski resort.
Low cloud and snow amplifying
the light so that when I first looked I thought
of aurora borealis, vision quests, dying stars.
Somehow driving always makes me think of the past,
as though the hypnotic taillights lined in front
were ringing you back, a grey tide of pavement
bearing you onto the shore of things you think
you'd rather forget, yet finger and turn over
in your pocket like sea glass. The endless curve of tarmac,
m-dashed and lined with hieroglyphs. Indicator. Lane dance.
The gravel shoulder reveals deep tire grooves, near misses.
You've got your hand on the gear shift, just waiting
for the moment to occur, snow on all sides, blue as a mirror.
You know you're home when the billboards advertise
places you know, on roads you know how to find.
Luminous cherry tomatoes of light.
The cars are all grey.

Expatriate

You recognize the walls now when you wake up.
The white, curtain-bright morning, the trees
a yellower green than in England—golden, even.
Last night on the patio, martinis going down easy,
there was no reason to believe you hadn't
always been camping in someone's living room,
shuttled over as a fixer-upper if there ever was one,
floundering, trading one country for another
in hopes that the equation for one man's meaning
can be duplicated. And isn't it strange?
How easy this becomes, putting your clothes
in new drawers, learning the order of new cupboards,
and even before you put out your hand there is another
extended, offering. And someone enters the room
and says, 'sorry, I need to grab this book off the table',
and 'would you like a cup of tea?' and then you have your tea
exactly as you always have, and for eight minutes
you do nothing but sip and watch the beach towels
on a clothesline, snapping in the golden green light.

There Are No Pretty Girls Here

There are no pretty girls here.
No girls appearing like green leaves
on bare branches. No girls of wit
or moody weather, deer legs disappearing

under breezy knee-length skirts, hair bridled
and plaited, practiced hands that know
their role without a mirror. No, there are
no pretty girls here. No shapeshifting

brilliance, eager laughter, small brass bells
that lure drinks from a wallet,
senses through a sieve. Inside pretty
girls there are beards of bees,

the slow bleaching silence of the Great Barrier Reef,
horses hitting panic-button gallops.
Perhaps they stayed home
today, laid their glamorous heads down

on white pillows and dreamt of rimless dark.
Go try another neighbourhood, another town;
see if there's a girl running barefoot down
a gravel drive, just waiting to show you fireflies

constellating an open field, the frothy gold
of her tanned stomach, the blade
she will open inside you once
you've forgotten everything

except her name; then be assured—
there are no pretty girls here.

"Commuter's Elimination Dance" is included with apologies to Michael Ondaatje.

"Newlywed" and "At a Country Pub in Avon" are for Guy Crawford.

"There Are No Pretty Girls Here" was inspired by a lyric fragment from the song 'Little Faith' by *The National.*

Some of these poems have previously appeared in *Carousel*, *CV2*, *Event*, *The Fiddlehead*, *Misunderstandings Magazine*, *Prairie Fire* and *PRISM International*. Others were published in the chapbook, *Coordinating Geometry* (The Emergency Response Unit, 2012). "Widow Fantasies" was anthologized in *Best Canadian Poetry in English 2011*; my thanks to the editors, Molly Peacock and Pricilla Uppal.

Thank-you hugs to Andrew Faulkner, Scott McDougall, Leigh Nash, Roger Nash, David Seymour, and Blair Trewartha who all contributed valuable notes and feedback on poems in various states of evolution over the past few years.

Thanks to Guy Crawford, my favourite person.

Huge thanks to Jim Johnstone for years of gin and tonics and much-needed kicks in the ass.

I would like to thank the Toronto Arts Council and the Ontario Arts Council for support during the writing of this book.

Julie Cameron Gray is originally from Sudbury, Ontario. She is the author of two poetry chapbooks, *Coordinating Geometry* [The Emergency Response Unit, 2012] and *The Distance Between Two Bodies* [Cactus Press, 2005]. Her poems have been published in *Carousel*, *CV2*, *Event*, *The Fiddlehead*, *Misunderstandings Magazine*, *Prairie Fire* and *PRISM International*. She lives in Toronto.